D0604691

UNEXPLAINED

AREA 51

BY TED MARTIN

WARNING
AREA 51
Restricted Area

It is unlawful to enter this area
without permission of the
Installation Commander.
Sec.21, International Security Act of 1950; 50 U.S.C.797

While on this installation all
personnel and the property
under their control are
subject to search.

USE OF DEADLY FORCE AUTHORIZED
AREA 51

TORQUE

Are you ready to take it to the extreme?
Torque books thrust you into the action-packed world
of sports, vehicles, mystery, and adventure. These books
may include dirt, smoke, fire, and dangerous stunts.
WARNING: read at your own risk.

Library of Congress Cataloging-in-Publication Data

Martin, Ted
 Area 51 / by Ted Martin.
   p. cm. -- (Torque. The unexplained)
 Includes bibliographical references and index.
 Summary: "Engaging images accompany information about Area 51. The combination of high-interest
subject matter and light text is intended for students in grades 3 through 7"-- Provided by publisher.
 ISBN 978-1-60014-642-8 (hardcover : alk. paper)
 1. Unidentified flying objects--Sightings and encounters--Nevada--Juvenile literature. 2. Area 51 (Nev.)--
Juvenile literature. 3. Air bases--Nevada--Juvenile literature. 4. Research aircraft--United States--Juvenile
literature. I. Title. II. Title: Area Fifty-one.
 TL789.5.N3M37 2012
 001.942--dc22   2011002257

This edition first published in 2012 by Bellwether Media, Inc.

Printed in the United States of America, North Mankato, MN.

080111   1187

CONTENTS

CHAPTER 1
SOMETHING TO HIDE?

In the 1950s, people began to see strange objects in a remote part of Nevada. They reported weird lights in the sky and **UFOs**. Many people linked the reports to a nearby United States military base called Groom Lake. Some people thought the military researched **aliens** and their technology there. Today, the base is called Area 51.

In 1974, a crew of **astronauts** traveled into space to take photos of Earth's surface. They were told not to take photos of Area 51. However, the astronauts accidentally took photos of the base. The **Central Intelligence Agency (CIA)** had the photos **classified**. What did the photos show? Did the government have something to hide?

Today, the CIA uses the name Area 51, but the base has been known by many other names over the years. They include Groom Lake, Dreamland, The Box, Watertown Strip, and Homey Airport.

IDENTITY CRISIS

Nevada

Area 51

CHAPTER 2

WHAT IS AREA 51?

Many people believe the B-2 Spirit was tested at Area 51. However, this has never been confirmed.

21070

8

Area 51 is a U.S. military base and airfield. It is located about 80 miles (129 kilometers) northwest of Las Vegas, Nevada. The base is part of the Nevada Test and Training Range. This is an area where the military tests new aircraft.

Area 51 was first used as a bombing range. It became a base to test aircraft in 1955. The military used it to test the U-2 spy plane and the SR-71 Blackbird. It was later used to test **stealth aircraft** such as the F-117 Nighthawk.

Many people believe that Area 51 is more than a test site. In 1947, the military responded to a UFO sighting in Roswell, New Mexico. They claim to have found only a **weather balloon**.

weather balloon

However, many people think the military found aliens and their spacecraft. They believe the military took what it found to Area 51. The base has been top secret ever since the crash.

RESEARCH AT AREA 51?

Some people believe that scientists at Area 51 have studied a wide range of alien technology. They think this research has led to better technology on our planet.

Technology

Anti-Gravity Device

Biotechnology

Computers

Energy Sources

Spacecraft

Stealth Technology

Superconductors

Description

One scientist claimed that he worked on an anti-gravity device at Area 51. This technology would remove the effect of Earth's gravity and allow objects to float in the air.

Many people think alien bodies have been studied at Area 51. They believe that this may have led to better biomedical technology for humans.

Computers advanced quickly after the 1950s. Some people think that alien technology was responsible.

Reports have claimed that the Area 51 spacecraft ran on an alien energy source called Element 115. Scientists may have studied this energy source to make new technology.

Humans developed spacecraft after the crash at Roswell. Some people think the technology came from alien spacecraft at Area 51.

The materials and shape of an aircraft can make it invisible to radar. Some people believe that the military got this technology from alien spacecraft.

Materials that move electricity better than standard conductors have been studied since the early 1900s. Advanced superconductors used in the 1950s and 60s may have come from alien technology.

CHAPTER 3
SEARCHING FOR ANSWERS

WARNING

AREA 51

Restricted Area

It is unlawful to enter this area without permission of the Installation Commander.
Sec.21, International Security Act of 1950; 50 U.S.C.797

While on this installation all personnel and the property under their control are subject to search.

USE OF DEADLY FORCE AUTHORIZED

AREA 51

Area 51 is heavily guarded. No one is allowed to take photographs near it. This has led to many **theories** about the base. Some people think the military hides alien technology there. The military denies these claims.

Air and space technology advanced at a quick pace after World War II. Some people think this can only be explained by access to alien technology. Did the military learn from alien spacecraft at Area 51? Could they have used alien technology to build new airplanes and spacecraft?

Another popular theory is that alien bodies are kept at Area 51. Some people believe that the aliens that crashed in Roswell lived for several weeks after the crash. They claim that the military asked the aliens questions. The military may also have performed **autopsies** on the bodies.

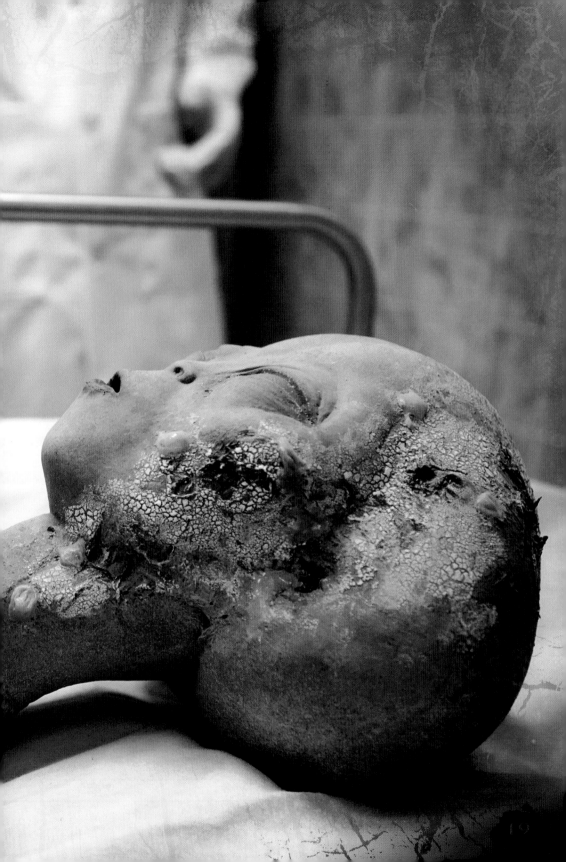

RELOCATED?

Area 51 has gained a lot of attention over the years. Some people think it is too well known. They believe that the alien bodies and spacecraft were moved to a new, secret location.

No one has found **evidence** that aliens or alien spacecraft are kept at Area 51. We only know that no one can go near the base. What is the military hiding? Is Area 51 just a base for testing aircraft? Or are other theories closer to the truth?

GLOSSARY

aliens—beings from other planets

astronauts—people who travel and work in space

autopsies—examinations of dead bodies; autopsies are performed to learn more about a life-form or why a life-form died.

Central Intelligence Agency (CIA)—a United States government agency that deals with spying and top secret government information

classified—kept secret from the public

evidence—physical proof of something

stealth aircraft—aircraft that uses advanced technology to hide from radar

theories—ideas that try to explain why something exists or happens

UFOs—unidentified flying objects; UFOs are often thought to be alien spacecraft.

weather balloon—a large balloon that is floated high in the atmosphere to take weather readings

TO LEARN MORE

AT THE LIBRARY

Grace, N.B. *UFO Mysteries*. Chanhassen, Minn.: Child's World, 2007.

Stewart, Gail B. *Area 51*. Farmington Hills, Mich.: KidHaven Press, 2009.

Wencel, Dave. *UFOs*. Minneapolis, Minn.: Bellwether Media, 2010.

ON THE WEB

Learning more about Area 51 is as easy as 1, 2, 3.

1. Go to www.factsurfer.com.

2. Enter "Area 51" into the search box.

3. Click the "Surf" button and you will see a list of related Web sites.

With factsurfer.com, finding more information is just a click away.

INDEX